Bowly Can't Do it YET

A Growth Mindset Story

by Angharad Davies

The Positive
Motherhood Project

First published in 2024 by The Positive Motherhood Project Ltd

www.bowlycan.com

© 2024 Angharad Davies

ISBN: 978-1-7390947-0-6

For my ever-so-supportive husband, Luis.
Thank you for always helping me see the
'not yet' when the big stones block my light.

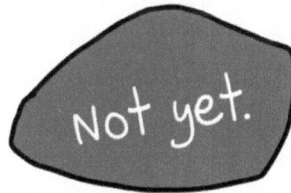

Not yet.

Hello there!

I can't seem to find my friend.
His name's Bowly McLight.
He's a little light-filled bowl.
We were supposed to meet up here.

Hold on.
I hear shouting.
I wonder...

Here you are, Bowly!
Was that you doing all that shouting?
I see you have a stone in there blocking out your light.
You normally get a stone when you feel angry, don't you?

YEAH.

It looks like you were trying to walk that tightrope.
Did you get angry because you felt like you couldn't do it?

Yet!

Who said that?
Was that you, Bowly?

—Nope.

Where did that sound come from?
Come on, let's take a look...

That's strange.
There's nothing here.
Oh well.

Why don't you try walking the tightrope again, Bowly?

— okey-dokey.

Ummm...

That's it, Bowly.
Keep going.

Hmph!

I can see that you're feeling angry again.
That stone seems to have grown too.

You're giving up.

Yet!

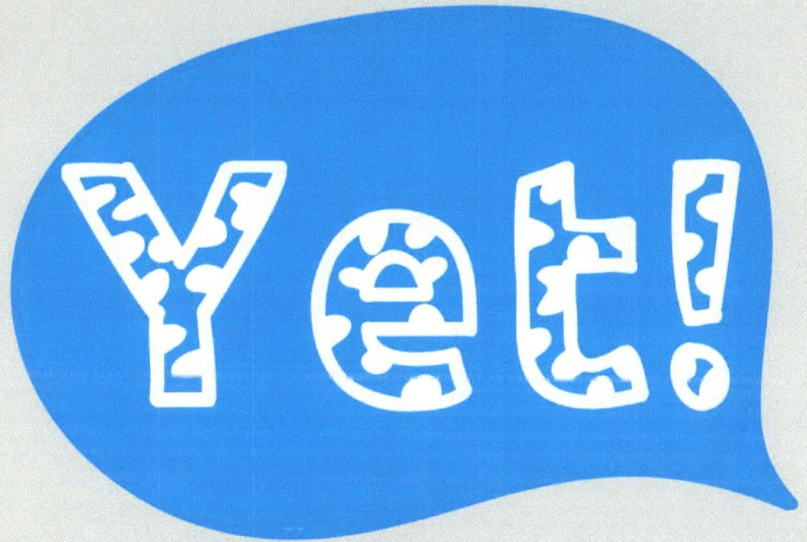

What? Again?
Who's there?

~ Huh?

Come on, Bowly.
Let's take a closer look...

That's really odd.
There's nothing here.
Maybe we just imagined it.
Never mind.

Hmmm...

Bowly, I think we should give that tightrope one more try.

Ummmm...

That's it.
Keep going.

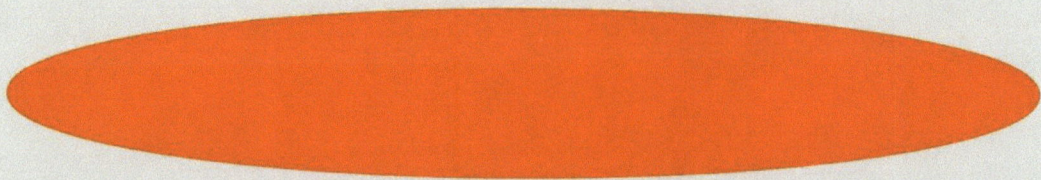

WOOOAH!

You're doing it, Bowly.
You're almost there.

Oh no!
You're stopping again.

You're giving up.

I can't do it.

Oh, Bowly.

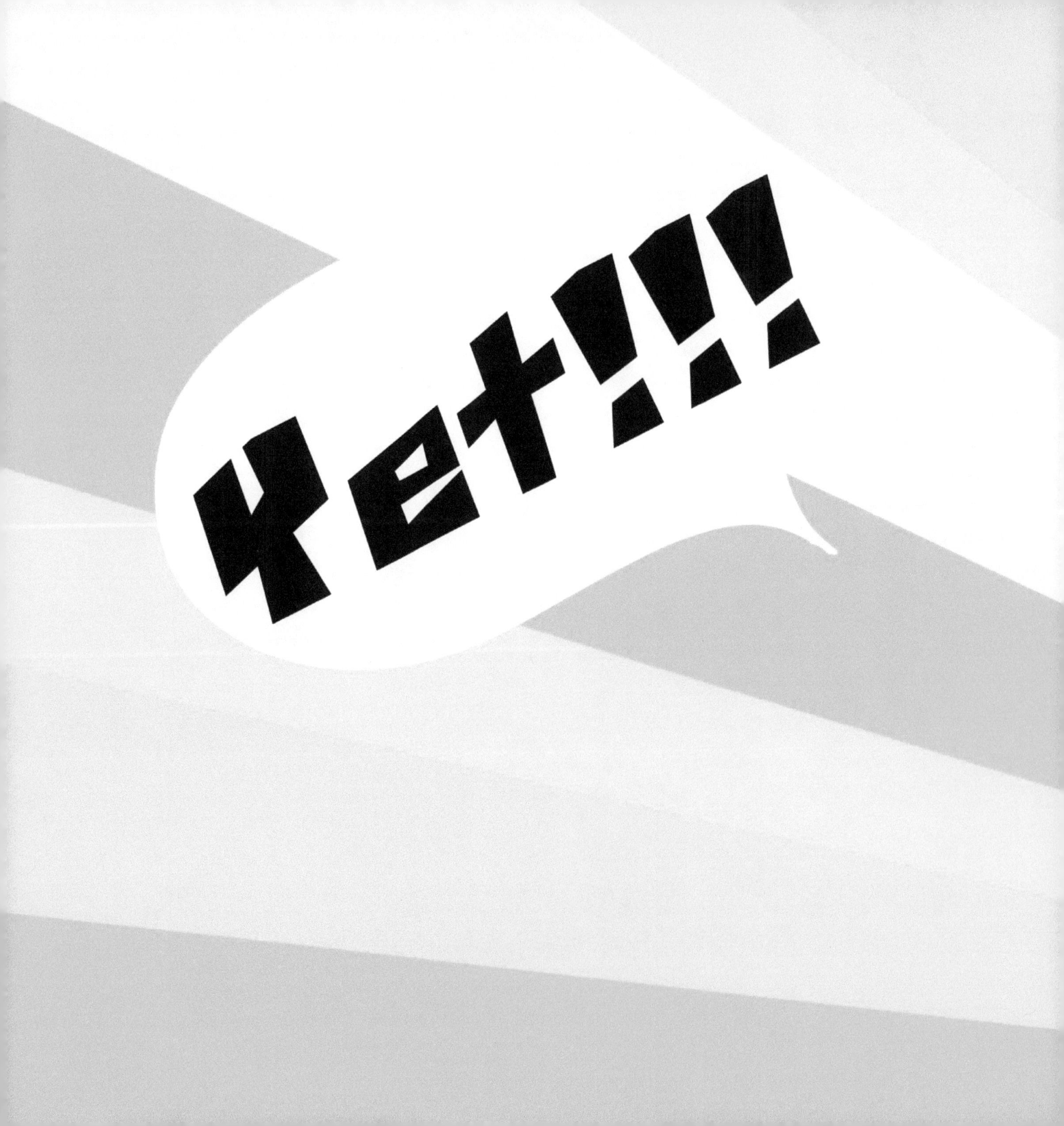
Yet!!!

Bowly, you didn't give up.
Look, your stone has shrunk!

You're still trying.
You're almost there.
Look, the stone has disappeared!

Wowee!
You did it, Bowly.
Your light is shining again!

I guess we won't get to the bottom of
that mysterious yet, though.
Never mind.

Come on, Bowly.
Show us your tightrope walk one last time.

Rah!

Yet!

Yet!

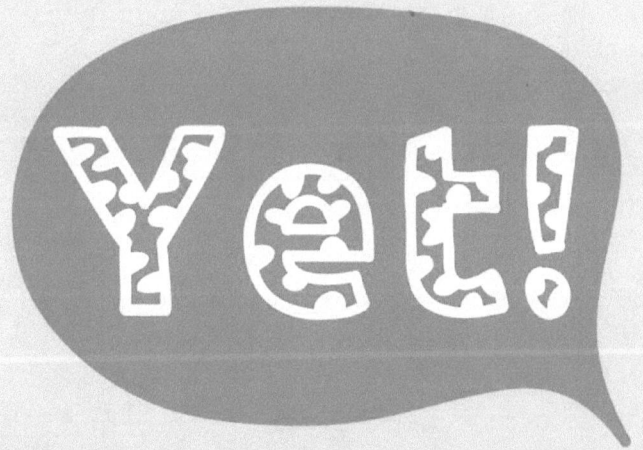

No matter how tough something gets,
It's never a never.
It's just a not yet.

Yet-tea

The story might be over, but Bowly has one last thing for you.

Make Bowly's tool come alive in the FREE video training

Take your very own Bowly with you wherever you go! Learn how to use the power of yet at home, at school and out and about.

If Bowly can... ...so can you!

www.bowlycan.com/f/yet

The transportable Bowly-in-the-hand move will be a game-changer for your child!
Easy and practical to use, before long your little one will be reminding you to use the power of yet!

About the author

Angharad Davies lives in the UK with her ever-so-supportive husband and her two amazing little boys.

After witnessing the magic of story in her own children for nurturing emotional intelligence and resilience, she decided to write her own.

Combining her knowledge from postgraduate qualifications in Psychology and Play Therapy with her children's love for humorous reads, Bowly McLight was born. With the help of her own children's story ideas and illustrations, Angharad is on a mission to deliver practical mindset and resilience tools to children through the power of story.

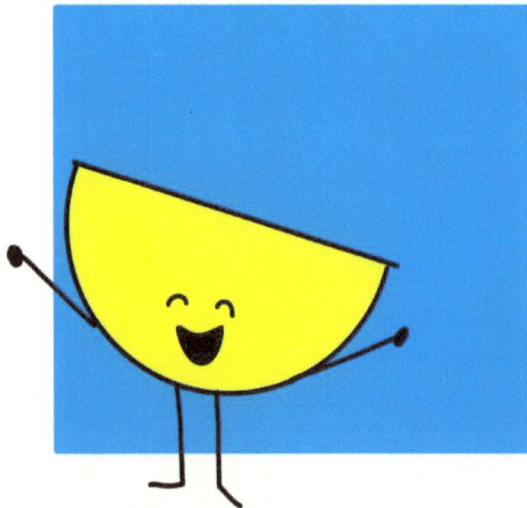

About Bowly

Bowly was inspired by the Hawaiian teaching of the Bowl of Light.

He is fun-loving and adores a challenge. He wears his big emotions on his sleeve and is on a mission to teach children everywhere the coolest of tools, so that they too can face anything life throws at them - even big dragons!

A new tool in every story

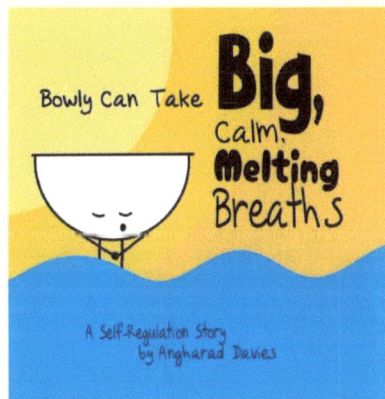

Bowly is covered in mud and feeling angry,
but he has just the right tool: his big, calm, melting breath.
There is just a bit more melting than he had anticipated!

A fun story to introduce children to a practical
and powerful breathing tool.
The perfect book for nurturing self-regulation and mindfulness.

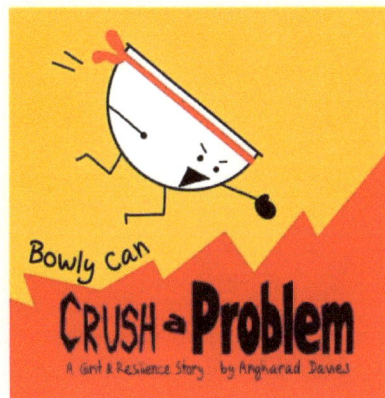

Bowly faces challenge after challenge, but never gives up.
He has a karate-chopping-problem-solving trick up his sleeve!
There's nothing that can stop him, except a dragon maybe.

A super fun story to teach children a powerful question
when faced with a problem: *"What's the hard part?"*
The perfect book to help nurture resilience and a
solution-focused mindset.

www.ingramcontent.com/pod-product-compliance
Lightning Source LLC
LaVergne TN
LVHW072108070426
835509LV00002B/77